HAL•LEONARD
INSTRUMENTAL
PLAY-ALONG

AUDIO ACCESS
INCLUDED

TRUMPET

Piazzolla Tangos

T0061415

To access audio visit:
www.halleonard.com/mylibrary

Enter Code
6530-9522-4506-7877

ISBN 978-1-4950-2842-7

DISTRIBUTED BY

CORPORATION
7777 W. BLUEMOUND RD. P.O. BOX 13819 MILWAUKEE, WI 53213

www.boosey.com
www.halleonard.com

AUSENCIAS
(The Absent)

TRUMPET

ASTOR PIAZZOLLA

EL VIAJE
(The Voyage)

TRUMPET

ASTOR PIAZZOLLA

CHANSON DE LA NAISSANCE
(Song of the Birth)
from FAMILLE D'ARTISTES

TRUMPET

ASTOR PIAZZOLLA

MILONGA
from A MIDSUMMER NIGHT'S DREAM

TRUMPET

ASTOR PIAZZOLLA

LIBERTANGO

TRUMPET

ASTOR PIAZZOLLA

LOS SUEÑOS
(Dreams)
from SUR

TRUMPET

ASTOR PIAZZOLLA

dim.

pp

OBLIVION

TRUMPET

ASTOR PIAZZOLLA

OUVERTURE
from FAMILLE D'ARTISTES

TRUMPET

ASTOR PIAZZOLLA

SENSUEL
(Sensual)
from A MIDSUMMER NIGHT'S DREAM

TRUMPET

ASTOR PIAZZOLLA

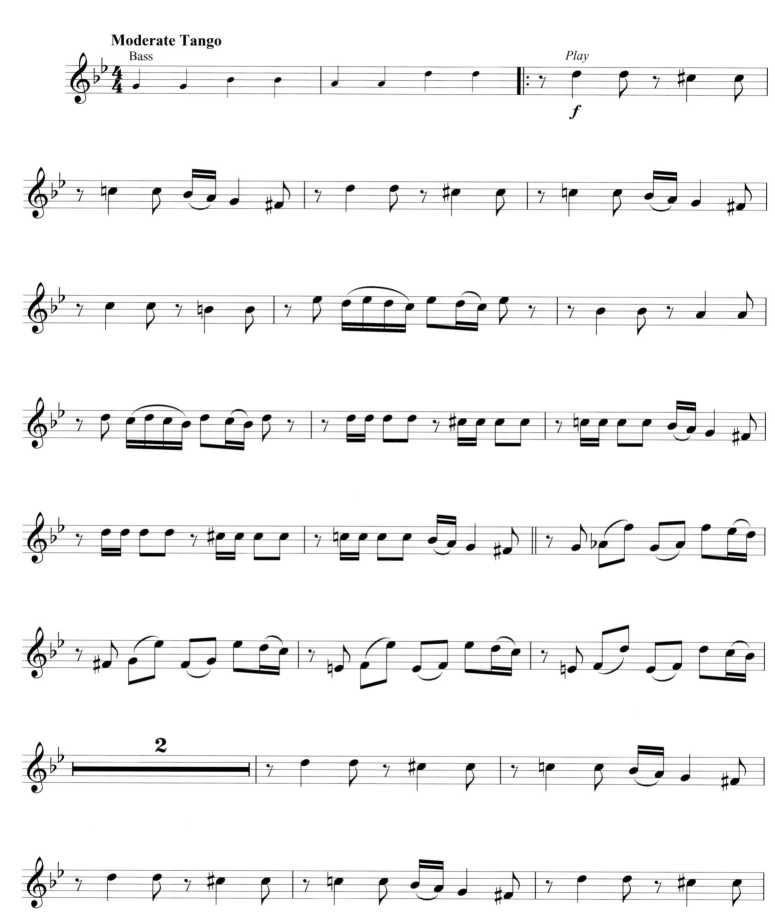

SENTIMENTAL
from FAMILLE D'ARTISTES

TRUMPET

ASTOR PIAZZOLLA

VUELVO AL SUR
(I'm Returning South)

TRUMPET

ASTOR PIAZZOLLA

SIN RUMBO
(Aimless)

TRUMPET

ASTOR PIAZZOLLA

STREET TANGO

TRUMPET

ASTOR PIAZZOLLA

21

TANGO FINAL
from FAMILLE D'ARTISTES

TRUMPET

ASTOR PIAZZOLLA